D0604241

TRACTORS

Aaron Carr

NO LONGER PROPERTY OF ANYTHINK RANGEVIEW LIBRARY DISTRICT

LET'S READ
AV2 BY WEIGL
ADDED VALUE · AUDIO VISUAL

www.av2books.com

AV² provides enriched content that supplements and complements this book. Weigl's AV² books strive to create inspired learning and engage young minds in a total learning experience.

Your AV² Media Enhanced books come alive with...

Audio
Listen to sections of the book read aloud.

Key Words
Study vocabulary, and complete a matching word activity.

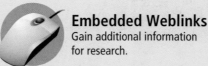

Video
Watch informative video clips.

Quizzes
Test your knowledge.

Embedded Weblinks
Gain additional information for research.

Slide Show
View images and captions, and prepare a presentation.

Try This!
Complete activities and hands-on experiments.

... and much, much more!

Go to **www.av2books.com**, and enter this book's unique code.

BOOK CODE

W226125

AV² **by Weigl** brings you media enhanced books that support active learning.

Published by AV² by Weigl
350 5th Avenue, 59th Floor
New York, NY 10118
Website: www.av2books.com   www.weigl.com

Copyright ©2014 AV² by Weigl
All rights reserved. No part of this publication may be reproduced, stored in a retrieval system, or transmitted in any form or by any means, electronic, mechanical, photocopying, recording, or otherwise, without the prior written permission of the publisher.

Library of Congress Control Number: 2013936159
ISBN 978-1-62127-381-3 (hardcover)
ISBN 978-1-62127-387-5 (softcover)

Printed in the United States of America in North Mankato, Minnesota
2 3 4 5 6 7 8 9 0 17 16 15 14 13

112013
WEP111113

Project Coordinator: Aaron Carr   Art Director: Terry Paulhus

Weigl acknowledges Getty Images as the primary image supplier for this title.

TRACTORS

CONTENTS

Tractors are big machines.
They make work easier for people.

There are many kinds of tractors. Some tractors are used on farms. Others are used to build roads.

Tractors come in different sizes. Some tractors are about the size of a truck.

The biggest tractor is 21 feet tall and weighs 45 tons.

Tractors can use tools
that do different jobs.
They can pull tillers, plows,
and hay balers.

Tractors have very big, powerful motors. These motors may be as powerful as 500 horses.

13

14

Tractors have a place
near the back called a cab.
This is where the driver sits.

Tractors are made
for different kinds of land.
Most tractors have wheels.

Some tractors have tracks.

The backhoe loader is a special kind of tractor. It has a bucket on the front and a scoop on the back. It is used to make buildings and roads.

Tractors can be very dangerous. They may have sharp blades, spinning parts, or hot motors. People should always be careful around tractors.

TRACTOR FACTS

These pages provide more detail about the interesting facts found in the book. They are intended to be used by adults as a learning support to help young readers round out their knowledge of each machine featured in the *Mighty Machines* series.

Pages 4–5

Tractors are big farm machines. Though they are similar to trucks, tractors are made to drive slowly and pull heavy loads. The word "tractor" comes from a Latin word meaning "to pull." People have used tractors for more than 140 years. The first tractors used steam-powered engines. They were used mostly for moving heavy objects. The first gasoline-powered tractors were made in the late 1800s. Today, tractors are used to make many farm jobs easier.

Pages 6–7

There are many different kinds of tractors. Tractors are used to do a wide range of jobs. In addition to farm work, construction workers use tractors to help them make buildings and roads. At airports, tractors are used to pull luggage carts to the airplanes. Workers in the military use special armored tractors to help them build camps and barriers.

Pages 8–9

Tractors come in different sizes. Small tractors may be used for mowing lawns, landscaping, and doing small jobs on farms. Large tractors are used for working in large farm fields. The largest farm tractor in the world is the Big Bud 747. It is 21 feet (6.4 meters) high and weighs 45 tons (40.8 metric tons). This tractor was made to plow huge cotton fields in California.

Pages 10–11

Tractors can pull tools that do different jobs. They can be equipped with a wide range of tools, which makes the tractor one of the most versatile pieces of equipment on many job sites. Farmers use tractors equipped with various attachments to help them plant, grow, and harvest their crops. Tillers tear up the soil, harrows make the ground smooth, seed spreaders plant the seeds, sprayers spray the crops, and hay balers chop and bundle the crops.

Tractors have very big, powerful motors. A motor's power is measured in horsepower. Horsepower was invented by an engineer named James Watt. He found that, on average, a horse could do 33,000 foot-pounds of work in one minute. This means a motor that can do the same amount of work in one minute is said to be 1 horsepower. The largest John Deere farm tractor has a 560-horsepower motor.

Tractors have a place near the back called a cab. Drivers operate all functions of the tractor from inside the cab. The driver's seat is the main part of the cab. Most tractors have an enclosure around the cab. This keeps the driver safe. The cab houses controls for speed, braking, and steering. They are located around the driver's seat. Mirrors and lights are often attached to the outside of the cab.

Tractors are made for different kinds of land. Many tractors have two large rear wheels and two small front wheels. Four wheel drive tractors have large wheels at the front and back. Other tractors use rolling tracks instead of wheels. Wheels offer better steering, but tracks give better traction.

The backhoe loader is a special kind of tractor. A backhoe loader is a tractor fitted with a bucket, called a front loader, on the front and a backhoe, or digger, on the back. Backhoe loaders are one of the most common kinds of modified tractors. They are very versatile machines that are used on many construction sites. The backhoe can dig holes and trenches, while the front loader can load dirt into a dump truck for removal.

Tractors can be very dangerous. Even the smallest tractors weigh thousands of pounds (kilograms). Their massive size and weight, along with their large wheels and sharp metal attachments, mean there are many potential dangers whenever tractors are around. Most tractors have safety features designed to keep the driver safe, such as seat belts, enclosed cabs, and roll bars. However, people should always exercise caution when working with tractors.

KEY WORDS

Research has shown that as much as 65 percent of all written material published in English is made up of 300 words. These 300 words cannot be taught using pictures or learned by sounding them out. They must be recognized by sight. This book contains 50 common sight words to help young readers improve their reading fluency and comprehension. This book also teaches young readers several important content words, such as proper nouns. These words are paired with pictures to aid in learning and improve understanding.

Page	Sight Words First Appearance
5	are, big, for, make, people, they, work
6	farms, kinds, many, of, on, others, some, to, used, there
9	a, about, and, come, different, feet, in, is, the
11	can, do, that
12	as, be, have, may, these, very
15	back, near, place, this, where
16	land, made, most
19	has, it
21	always, around, or, parts, should

Page	Content Words First Appearance
5	machines, tractors
6	roads
9	sizes, tons, truck
11	hay balers, jobs, plows, tillers, tools
12	horses, motors
15	cab, driver
16	tracks, wheels
19	backhoe loader, bucket, buildings, front, roads, scoop
21	blades, motors

MEDIA ENHANCED BOOKS
AV² BY WEIGL™
ADDED VALUE • AUDIO VISUAL

Check out www.av2books.com for activities, videos, audio clips, and more!

The AV² Collection

1 Go to www.av2books.com.

2 Enter book code. | W 2 2 6 1 2 5 |

3 Fuel your imagination online!

www.av2books.com